I0148884

ALOVEDLIFE

AN ABSOLUTE LOVE PUBLISHING SPECIAL EDITION
VOLUME 1

CONSCIOUSLY CREATE A LIFE YOU LOVE

Almost a

HUNDRED

contributors

DOZENS

of publications

ONE MISSION:

to create and publish projects
promoting goodness in the world

ALOVEDLIFE

A PUBLICATION OF
ABSOLUTE LOVE PUBLISHING

Publisher
Caroline A. Shearer

Editor
Sarah Hackley

Ambassador
Denise Thompson

Intentional Living

Elevated Action

Conscious Connection

Sacred Self-Care

FRONT COVER PHOTO BY HANNAH VEXIL NELSON

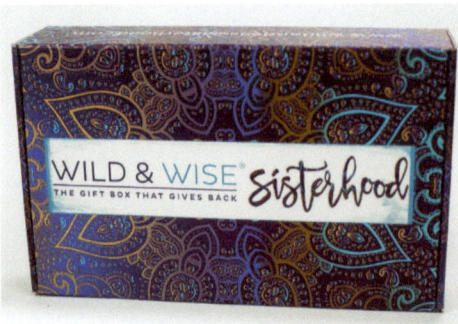

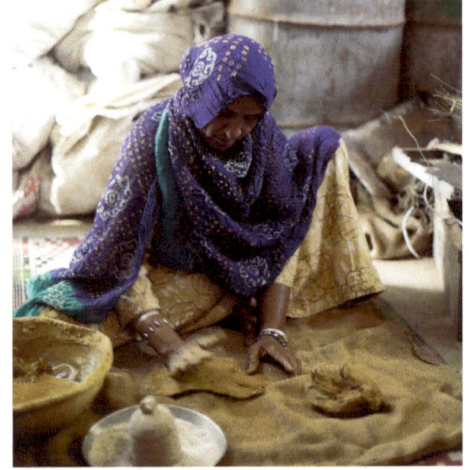

LOVE ALOVEDLIFE?

Welcome to the inaugural edition of ALOVEDLIFE, a book-magazine hybrid designed to help you consciously create a life you love. With evergreen content on Intentional Living, Elevated Action, Conscious Connection, and Sacred Self-Care, the tools and wisdom in ALOVEDLIFE will uplift and enhance your life so you can be your happiest and most fulfilled.

And we are **just getting started**! Find additional ALOVEDLIFE editions, pre-order options so you always have the latest content, and much more, including our selection of books and min-e-books™, in our online store: www.absolutelovepublishing.com/shop.

> Always remember you are braver than you believe, stronger than you seem, smarter than you think, and twice as beautiful as you'd ever imagined.
> - Rumi

Manifesting through Affirmations

CAROLINE A. SHEARER

I'm going to let you in on a secret. The main reason people suffer from a lack of money or love or health in their lives is that they do not value themselves – not really, not when you get down into those little crevices where doubts and criticisms live.

We believe we have made too many mistakes. We believe everyone else is doing things so much better. We think our flaws (hidden as we may keep them) make us unworthy of love or acceptance or a happy life. We think our successes aren't as valid as they really are; we make excuses for how we were able to win rather than claim our success outright.

Sure, on the whole, we may love ourselves. Sure, in principle we may love others – and even the whole world. But those nagging critiques are always there, just waiting for the opportunity to prey on our higher vibrations. It is those nefarious little bits of energy that keep us in our patterns of lack, insist we only deserve "so much", create new expenses to meet our increases in income so that we never get too far ahead (of ourselves), create new problems in our relationships so we are never "too happy", or create health issues so we never feel truly in the clear.

We must address this. We must value ourselves fully and completely if we are to blossom into the boundless beings we are and do so while enjoying the abundance and joy that is our birthright.

Do whatever you need to do, today, to delete those voices. Write them down on a piece of paper and burn them. Yell at them to stop. Delete them from your consciousness, just like you would an errant phrase in an email. And then move on. It's not easy; it's actually hard work. But it is doable with effort. And you can do it.

Working with Affirmations

As you work on deleting the negative voices, you'll now be left with a void. This is where the power of affirmations can enter. We can add positive self-talk to replace the negative self-talk.

A lot of people try to use affirmations and then quickly abandon them because the results don't come quickly enough or the process simply doesn't stick with their soul. That doesn't mean affirmations don't work. It means we need to work affirmations better.

Using Our Emotions

The key to the successful use of affirmations is the introduction of true emotion, because the emotions you feel are what will create the intended reality.

A lot of people try to use affirmations and then quickly abandon them because the results don't come quickly enough or the process simply doesn't stick with their soul. That doesn't mean affirmations don't work. It means we need to work affirmations better.

When we say words that have no meaning to us, they will create no new reality for us. We must resonate with our words through the pull of our emotions. In other words, if an affirmation seems too "unreal", you won't be able to achieve it.

When this happens, you can 1. work on believing an affirmation and/or 2. work on a more precise affirmation for your belief system. To this end, I encourage the use of tiered affirmations to help reach a point of true resonance in your heart and mind.

For example, let's take money:

1. I have $500k I can spend freely.

or

2. I am capable of having/securing $500k to spend freely.

See the difference?

If you are ready to believe that you have the money already, then the first affirmation is the one for you. If there is still doubt in your heart or in your mind, start with the second affirmation and build that part of your belief system first. Convince yourself that you are capable. Once you feel you are capable, then you can transition to the higher-level affirmation.

This same idea can be applied to any area where you feel doubt or insecurity:

I am worthy of a loving, respectful, passionate relationship.

I am in a loving, respectful, passionate relationship.

I can choose to have an abundant mindset.

I have an abundant mindset.

I am capable of securing a well-paying, fulfilling job.

I have a well-paying, fulfilling job.

My skills, thoughts, and actions can help bring me financial abundance.

My skills, thoughts, and actions are providing me financial abundance.

My body is capable of incredible health and vitality.

I am experiencing incredible health and vitality.

I know I can live an independent life with ample resources.

I am living an independent life with ample resources.

What you probably will find is that in some areas of your life, you'll want to shoot straight for the top with your preferred affirmations, and then in other areas, it might take several steps to get up to a higher level. I want to emphasize: work with whatever affirmations feel right to you. There is no "right" way, only what works! And just like if you were working toward a marathon, train yourself. Train yourself to rise.

Keep in mind, too, that it may or may not be in your best interest to heal every single flawed belief you have, all at one time. We're in this life to learn,

> Keep in mind, too, that it may or may not be in your best interest to heal every single flawed belief you have, all at one time.

and processing what we learn takes time. This is why it's so important to personalize your affirmations for your life, your "story". Tweak them until they serve as a bridge between where you are now and where you want to be.

And remember, too, we never, ever have the whole story. Our journey here is a magical and mysterious one. We can understand our life theme and recognize soulmates and unlock many universal principles, but we can never know it all. And believe it or not, that is a good thing!

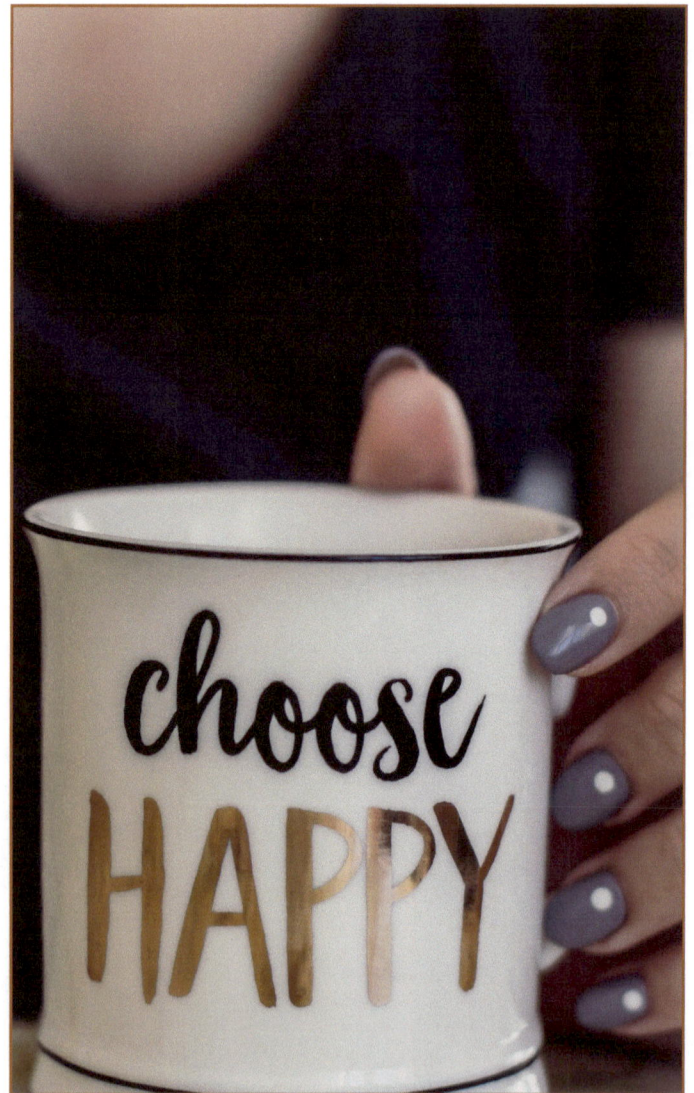

Adapted from Raise Your Financial Vibration: Tips and Tools to Embrace Your Infinite Spiritual Abundance, a min-e-book™

From *Personal Power through Awareness*
by Sanaya Roman

What is a commitment to yourself?

Some of you think it means using your will power to force yourself to live that vision of who you think you should be. You may feel that once you have decided to do something, you must stand inflexibly by that decision. Almost all of the resolutions you make about how you will act involve projecting your present-time self into a future time. That means making decisions for a time that has not yet arrived. Making a commitment to yourself is being in present time, acknowledging that you have enough sense of self to do what is right at this moment. It is trusting yourself, knowing you do not have to wake up and tell yourself how you will be, how you will handle things; you do not have to worry about three weeks from today or a year from now. It is knowing that you will not be the same person at that future time, that you will be wiser and more evolved. It is important to plan and visualize what you want from the future, but then relax and trust your future self.

Clear the Path
to Your
HIGHER PURPOSE

Lisa Capri

Are you embodying your highest and greatest purpose? Are you living in harmony with your desires? Or does it feel like you're constantly adjusting your compass and always on the outside of that elusive "flow" feeling the self-help experts tell us to find?

Even when we have a sense of our highest and greatest purpose and make decisions that bring us closer to it, we still can get sidetracked. We run from our highest purpose for all sorts of reasons: fear of failure, fear of success, fear of commitment, fear of change. You name it. But one piece of this puzzle that knowledge can help us avoid is Shiny Object Syndrome (SOS).

Shiny Object Syndrome

While the term SOS may have been coined originally for impulse shoppers who relentlessly pursue material goods, SOS can affect our ability to make any of the kinds of decisions that bring us closer to our highest and best selves because it affects how we spend our resources. By resources, I mean time, energy, money, and spirit. SOS affects our ability to make conscious, intentional decisions about the activities or ventures we choose to spend our resources on, which ultimately dictates whether or not we live in alignment with what we really want in life.

People who are highly motivated, curious, love to learn new things, and enjoy starting new projects or turning ideas into reality are the most likely to be afflicted by SOS. At first glance, the qualities on that list seem positive. After all, what could be so bad about being motivated and passionate about learning or getting involved in new (ad)ventures? For people with SOS tendencies, it means constantly chasing *novelty*, the next big thing ... the figurative shiny new object.

For entrepreneurs, this might be reflected in a steady stream of unfinished projects, abandoned marketing strategies, or the latest tech gadget rather than the monotony of repetitive actions required to achieve success in the long term. As a serial entrepreneur and someone who loves to learn new skills, I'm a textbook case of Shiny Object Syndrome. SOS has gotten me into trouble time and time again. Just as I start learning to avoid taking on too many projects at once, I inevitably come across an opportunity or learning curve that I *just* can't resist, and I get sucked down a rabbit hole, sometimes not coming up for air for several months ... until the next shiny new thing comes along. I have a tendency to think I can do several things at once, do them well, and that somehow there won't be any negative consequences as long as I just give it my all! This is almost always a recipe for disaster, or at least arrested development.

Is this starting to sound familiar?

SOS is very common amongst entrepreneurs and creatives, but you don't have to be an entrepreneur or a creative to get stuck in a pattern of SOS behavior. SOS isn't so much

DO YOU EXPERIENCE SOS?

- **Do you struggle with committing to a project or venture long enough to see it through to the finish line?**

- **Do you find yourself getting excited about a new project or venture only to lose interest in it the moment a new opportunity comes your way?**

- **Do you have multiple unfinished projects, even though you feel passionate about each one of them?**

- **Do you constantly change your focus or career path to see what "sticks" — all in an effort to find your life's purpose or live at your highest potential?**

about having multiple interests or passions, but rather what can happen when we do — whether our actions are taking us toward or away from our highest purpose. For all of us, SOS can manifest in many of life's spheres, whether we're seeking the emotional high of something or someone new or we're more excited about the initial discovery process than planning for the viability of the shiny new object.

What SOS Looks Like

For the sake of illustration, let's take two women, Patricia and Nancy:

Patricia loves crafting and sells crafts from her online shop while working her full-time job as a dance instructor. She also performs in a band every Friday night. Lately Patricia has taken an interest in portrait photography and has purchased professional photography equipment. She thinks she might be able to work less if photography could replace her dancing and singing income. She purchased the equipment three months ago but still hasn't had the time to learn how to use it, since she's been pulling a lot of hours at the dance studio, creating new crafts for her upcoming craft fair, and rehearsing with the band. She sometimes spends hours watching YouTube tutorials on photography late at night.

Nancy is a stay-at-home mom. She's always had a side hustle to earn extra income for the household, but she never sticks to one thing long enough for any of the side businesses to take off. Her side businesses turn into expensive hobbies. Last year, she dabbled with three different home-based business opportunities but quickly got bored with each of them after only a few weeks. When she starts a new side venture, she gets really excited and passionate about it, and that's all her husband, children, and friends hear about for weeks, until she gets bored and starts chasing something new.

Are you a Patricia or a Nancy? I've been both! I've alternated over the years, and sometimes when the SOS gets really bad, I've been both at the same time. If you're any version of Patricia or Nancy, what can you do about it?

CROP

Avoiding the shiny new objects that present themselves as distractions from our highest path can be as simple as remembering another acronym: CROP. Much like taking a photo and zooming in to what's most important, when presented with yet another shiny object we can choose to apply CROP to put our focus on what aligns with our highest purpose.

CROP is my self-invented criteria to help me make more informed, more intentional decisions. Here's how it works:

C

"C" stands for "clan" or "customer". If you're an entrepreneur, ask yourself if this new product or venture is something your customer really wants. Entrepreneurs often get excited about something that's trending and then FOMO (fear of missing out) kicks in. But in the rush to implement it, they don't take the time to assess whether this trend truly vibes with their company values and that of their customers. If you're not an entrepreneur, use the word "clan" in the context of your loved ones. If you take on this new activity or venture, how will it affect them? What will they get out of it? Consequently, what do they stand to lose if it doesn't pan out?

R

"R" stands for "resources". Before you reach out to that new shiny object, consider the resources you have available in time, money, energy, and spirit. Will you be depleting any one of these without a clear and *specific* game plan to replenish it? We like to think of ourselves as superheroes, with the ability to take on multiple demanding tasks at once, but realistically not everything will live up to the image we had in our minds.

O

"O" stands for "open", as in how many open projects you have running at once. Look seriously at how many unfinished projects there are in your business or in your home right now. Oftentimes, the answer to this question will produce a knee-jerk reaction that will result in you stepping away from the shiny object so you can forge ahead on your higher path.

P

"P" stands for "pause". Before you grab that new, pretty, shiny thing, take a breather. Allow the idea, opportunity, or venture to marinate, even for just a few days. Keep a journal to jot down the ideas or opportunities as they come so you'll feel like you're taking action in the short term, while still giving yourself the liberty to think things through before you jump.

At this point, you've made it through the four elements of CROP. Now, with the benefit of your thoughtful preparation, you'll either know the answer already or you can run it through CROP once again with the additional information in place.

There will always be shiny new objects on the path to living your best life and reaching your highest self. Are these gifts from the universe or blocks along your way? With CROP in hand, you can feel confident in your decisions and give yourself the best gift of all: the awareness that you have come to decision-making with purpose and intention.

And, hey, the next time a shiny new object comes knocking at your door, say hello! But take a while to get to know it before you invite it inside for coffee and cake.

Lisa Capri has owned and operated businesses in various fields for more than 15 years. She is the host of the *Raise Your Frequency Podcast*, a weekly show that tackles productivity and lifestyle habits for entrepreneurs. Lisa is obsessed with creating systems to get laser-focused on business goals while continuing to grow in one's personal life. Visit her at lisacapri.com.

FUNDAMENTALS of *Vibration*

I remember when I was a child, sitting on the grass with a friend, and I distinctly could feel the earth vibrating. I asked, "Can you feel that? Do you feel that?" over and over to my friend, with whom I wanted to share the experience. Even after I described it and after repeated attempts, she couldn't feel anything, but I was positive I did. I didn't realize at the time, but that was my first recognizable experience with the power of vibration.

As the years have gone by, I have come to realize how important vibration is to our life experience and how harnessing the power of vibration can improve our lives dramatically. Like a tool in our pocket, an understanding of vibration can uplift, ease, protect, endear, clear, etc. – anything we would like. And the more we choose to use our understanding of vibration for good, the higher our own vibration grows and the better human life we can experience.

But first, let's understand vibration.

What do I mean by vibration?

We first have to start with the understanding that **everything is energy**. The chair you're sitting on, the building you're in, the dog barking down the street, the flowers growing outside the window, and the thoughts going through your head. All of it is energy.

The earth does indeed vibrate, as do all parts in it, on it, and around it – including us. However, we do not have to physically feel it to harness it. If we want to utilize this energy to our highest and greatest benefit, we can begin to recognize that **everything has a frequency**. Generally speaking, lower, denser vibrations are more "earthly" and move more slowly, and higher, lighter frequencies are more "spiritual" and move more quickly. Most of us operate with an earthly frequency, with occasional moments of a more spiritual nature. The highest among us are able to resonate more closely with a spiritual frequency, while also remaining grounded.

Our goal is not to be a completely spiritual frequency, as that is what we are when we are on the "other side", and, after all, we have chosen to be on earth. However, we can choose to move toward higher frequencies more often in order to have a smoother, more fulfilling life. We can blend our earthly, human beings with higher dimensional energies that are in alignment with our souls.

We can begin to achieve higher frequencies by recognizing the pattern of **"like attracts like"**. More than just a saying, this is an energetic law. Frequencies are attracted to similar frequencies. We resonate at a higher frequency when we raise our vibration, and, therefore, attract higher-level experiences.

Ever notice how some people seem incredibly "lucky"? Or always have prosperity? Or how the people who complain (at work, in school, in organizations) seem to find each other? Or how some people have one run of bad "luck" after another? This is a function of similar vibrations attracting each other. If you are new to this concept, this is an excellent way to begin to see it in action, and if you're a longtime student, it's always a good

Excerpted from
Raise Your Vibration,
a min-e-book™
by Caroline A. Shearer

reminder. Look around yourself and see the patterns. They are there. Once you see the patterns, you can consciously choose which ones are right for you. (If you are wondering about your own vibration, look to your closest relationships and your environment for insight.)

It's important to be aware that *the stronger your spiritual consciousness* – your connection with the universal oneness – *the less you will be affected by lower vibrations*. They simply will not impact you in ways they had before. This is because, on a certain level, you are energetically aware that you are more than/beyond the earthly experience. In truth, it is the ego that allows us to be affected by lower vibrations in the first place, but as releasing the ego is a many lifetimes process for us, the rules of vibration are eminently important for us to utilize. What this means is, the more you work on creating a higher vibration and more spiritual consciousness, the more frequently undesirable influences will simply fall away from your life.

Principle: On the whole, humans are on an upward track for increasing their vibration. In fact, right now, we are breaking through incredible boundaries and seeing a rapid evolution of mass consciousness.

Principle: The highest vibrations – and our goals – are love and gratitude. Pure, absolute love and gratitude for everyone, ourselves, and everything. Feeling these pure emotions is our natural state; the rest is conditioning.

It's important to be aware that the stronger your spiritual consciousness – your connection with the universal oneness – the less you will be affected by lower vibrations.

We are *all* attuned, empathetic, and telepathic. It is only our openness and receptiveness to these abilities that varies. As we raise our own vibration, we will more easily tap into these experiences.

Principle: Moving faster does not raise your vibration; *being* slower does. When we are in a centered, peaceful, "available" state, the vibration of all we are transforms to a high frequency.

Principle: We are *all* attuned, empathetic, and telepathic. It is only our openness and receptiveness to these abilities that varies. As we raise our own vibration, we will more easily tap into these experiences.

Vibration Fundamentals

Everything is energy.
We all have a frequency.
Like attracts like.

What's the difference between higher and lower vibration?

When we operate at a higher vibration, we have positive thoughts, and we attract positive people and activities. We also attract synchronicities, which allow us to go with the flow of the universe and guide us on our highest and greatest path. We are able to enjoy clearer intuition, peace, and happiness. Higher vibration lives still challenge us to grow, but our growth comes more smoothly and with greater ease.

Higher vibration = more positive

When we operate at a lower vibration, we have negative thoughts over and over again, and we attract negative people, activities, irritations, and drama into our lives. We also tend to have lower energy and are more susceptible to depression, which is like living in a cloud of denser, lower energies. Lower vibration lives are challenging lives filled with more struggles.

Lower vibration = more negative

Why do we choose to raise our vibration?

1. Raising our vibration allows us to resonate at a higher frequency and attract a life benefitting our highest and greatest good.

We all have a highest and greatest purpose in this humanly experience. Your life theme, the reason you are here on earth, could be learning greater love or instilling self-reliance or finding peace, among other things. Depending on your vibration, you will work on learning your theme regardless, but the higher your vibration, the higher your level of learning.

For example, to put this in simplistic terms: if your life theme was to learn another language, a low vibration result might be a rudimentary grasp of the language. If you have a moderate vibration level, you will learn the language but struggle and perhaps never fully feel confident in it. When you vibrate highly, you would then be able to master the language, be fluent, and be confident, enough so to teach to others. All three involve the language, but only the high vibration path results in mastery.

This is what I mean when discussing how your life will flow based on vibration. Do you want to be stuck at the bottom always struggling? Do you want to get lost in the middle with the crowd? Or do you want to vibrate highly and shine, fulfilling the highest and greatest use of your lifetime and skills and self?

2. Raising our vibration helps us more clearly receive communication and messages from God, angels, and other high-frequency spiritual entities. As humans, we are not able to see the entire picture on our own. Being able to access guidance can improve our perception of situations dramatically, and therefore allow us to improve our situations dramatically.

3. Raising our vibration allows us to receive accurate intuitive information from our higher selves. We have more information than we realize, and in addition to being helpful, connecting with our higher selves is soothing and reaffirming.

4. Being in tune with the vibrations of others can help us make better relationship choices, life choices, and career choices. This is what it's all about, really. We always have options, we always have choices. Which do we pick? Who do we pick? Each leads us down a different path that ultimately creates the complicated maze of our lives, but realizing we have so much control over the quality of those paths is the instrumental factor in how much we progress and enjoy our lives.

Consistently choosing activities and thoughts that raise our vibration will re-wire our brains so that these actions and thoughts become more natural to us. The more we do it, the better we get!

What Is Your *Resonant Frequency?*

By Sue Elliott

The Value of Knowing and Emitting Your Own Personal Power Signal

We each have what I call a resonant frequency: a strong energy that we emit naturally. When we're "feeling like ourselves" (as opposed to feeling "off"), we're experiencing what it's like to *be* in our resonant frequency. For some people, their resonant frequency is peace. For others, it's enthusiasm or appreciation.

Now, you might be thinking: *Those are just emotions.* And, of course, they are. But while we are capable of feeling the full spectrum of emotions, we each have just one resonant frequency, which also could be called our personal power signal.

I've known for quite a while that my own resonant frequency is *joy.* When I am in a joyful state, I act like a tuning fork, attuning other people to the vibration of joy. I have seen my joy affect people who are sitting, standing, and even working within a 30-foot radius around me, and I've found that it can affect people on the other side of the country and the world, too.

Our resonant frequencies are contagious. A person who's emitting the resonant frequency of peace can bring profound peace to a space and to the people and other creatures within that space. Resonant frequencies are that powerful! And this ability to affect others is only one of the many effects that come from emitting our own personal power signal.

What Kind of Power?

A quick explanation of the kind of power we are (and are not) talking about here: When most people think of power, they think of it as something we can wield over others, something we can use to get other people to do what we want them to do. And yes, that's the form of power that has been dominant on our planet for a long time. But there's another kind of power — what I call *authentic power.* It isn't "power over". Instead, it's "power to", as in power to affect massive change in the world, power to accomplish great things, power to

Not only do you *feel* better, you also can be a force for good wherever you go simply by showing up as you!

create masterpieces.

This power comes from within. It doesn't require aggression, domination, or any sort of control over others. But it *does* require self-control and self-awareness.

Accessing This Power

We each have access to this massive, beautiful power — the power to create, manifest, thrive, and shine — and one really fun way to tap into it is to discover and then emit our resonant frequency. When we emit this frequency, people can feel our authenticity. They can feel what some call our "soul signature". It's a potent expression of our unique self.

Most people around us will find this energy intriguing… and *very* attractive. There are numerous reasons for this. For one, our resonant frequencies are *positive*, so they help to attune others to more positive energy states. In addition, when others are in the presence of our authentic power, it helps them feel stirrings within — on a deep cellular and soul level — of their own authentic power.

Discovering Your Resonant Frequency

So you already know *my* resonant frequency is joy. The question is: What's yours?

Did an emotion or feeling state pop into your mind when you read that question (or while you've been reading thus far)? If it did, that's great. If not, you can discern your resonant frequency pretty easily. Let's start by asking some questions since questions are a powerful tool for accessing truth.

Can you remember a time when you felt really powerful? Again, we're not talking about "power over" here; we're talking about "power to". You might remember a time when you felt really powerful at work (perhaps you gave a presentation that totally rocked). Or maybe you remember feeling really powerful while playing a sport (perhaps a situation from childhood comes to mind).

Once you've got the situation, it's time to explore it. Take some time to remember the scene in as much detail as you can. Put yourself back into that moment, looking through your own eyes. See it. Hear it. Smell the smells. Taste the tastes. Feel the physical sensations.

Are you totally immersed in the moment? Good. Now check in and notice: What emotion (or combination of emotions) are you feeling?

You might notice that you're feeling calm or centered. Or you might be feeling kind or playful *and* generous. Resonant frequencies don't have to be just one thing. There are far more resonant frequencies than emotions because some people's resonant frequencies can best be described as hybrids, like *gentle compassion* or *hopeful optimism*. See how specific you can get in identifying yours.

Tune in to Your Frequency

Once you've discovered your resonant frequency, it's time to have some fun with it! Let's start by tuning in to it. This is remarkably like tuning in to a radio station, except instead of looking for a certain frequency on an external device, you're looking for a feeling within your own body.

How? Actually, there are lots of ways to attune yourself to your resonant frequency. You might call up a memory of a time when you were experiencing that feeling. Or, for example, if your resonant frequency is tenderness, you might gently pet a cat or even look at photos online of babies and puppies. If your resonant frequency is peace, perhaps the sound of a fountain will help you attune to it. As you're reading this, it's very likely that a variety of inspirations are popping into your mind for different ways to tune in to your unique frequency.

Once you have tuned in to your resonant frequency, spend some time there. Allow yourself to marinate in this energy. While you're soaking in it, gently notice: What does it light up within you? Is it affecting you physically? Are you experiencing sensations anywhere in your body? Is it adjusting your posture? Are you smiling? What else are you noticing on a physical level?

Now check in mentally. As you bask in your resonant frequency, is it bringing up memories of other times when you were strongly emitting this energy? Take some time to really savor those memories. Roll around in them! Notice what else is coming to mind.

Now check in emotionally. Sure, you're feeling the emotion that *is* your resonant frequency. But what else are you feeling? For instance, are you feeling freer? More expansive? More potent?

Also notice what you are experiencing on a spiritual level. Does it feel easier to connect with your intuition? Are you feeling inspired? Do you feel more in alignment with God/Source/the Infinite?

Day-to-Day Uses

As you've probably gathered, the more you experience and express your resonant frequency, the more powerful you'll be. Being in this vibration helps you align with your purpose and passion, as well as get into the flow state. So how can you experience being in your resonant frequency more and more within your day-to-day life?

Here's a practical example: Let's say you're deciding what to eat for lunch. In my case, since joy is my resonant frequency, I'm going to get into a joyful state before I decide what to eat (and also where to eat, if I'm going out to lunch). Once the food is on my plate, I'm going to give joyful appreciation for the food, and I'm going to consciously connect with the food and ask it to help me amplify my resonant frequency of joy. Ideally, if I find myself feeling anything other than joyful during the meal — for instance, if I start feeling annoyed — I am going to stop eating until I come back into alignment with my resonant frequency. This way, the food helps me to more fully and deeply embody joy.

Of course, this works for lots more than just food! You can take the same approach with everything, from doing the dishes and paying bills to writing an email message, deciding what to wear, walking the dog, and giving someone a hug.

As you practice with these "little" day-to-day activities, it will become easier to remain steady and keep emitting your resonant frequency during more "challenging" circumstances, such as while giving a presentation at work, when your child is having a meltdown in a department store, or when you arrive at the airport and find out your flight has been delayed. Just imagine how helpful a resonant frequency of calm, compassion, or peace would be in any of those situations. It helps to center and balance not only you but also those around you as you spread more calm, compassion, or peace.

That's the beauty and the power of expressing your resonant frequency: Not only do you feel better, you also can be a force for good wherever you go simply by showing up as you!

I would love to hear how this process and awareness plays out for you. Please connect with me and share your personal experiences via my website: www.JoyfulPower.com.

Through her transformative work with business leaders, as well as her writing and media appearances, Sue Elliott has helped millions of people experience more joy, ease, peace, and personal power. Sue currently helps exceptional CEOs supercharge their power by connecting them with Divine guidance (www.JoyfulPower.com).

TAKE CHARGE OF YOUR

Wealth Signature

BASED ON RAISE YOUR FINANCIAL VIBRATION, A MIN-E-BOOK™

Did you know? You have a wealth signature. But, before you grab a piece of paper and try a fancy new way of signing your name, this is not the same signature we use for our electronic documents, texts, emails, paperwork, and personal notes. This is an invisible and potent energetic vibration directly connected to your financial well-being. It is the essence or the vibration that attracts your financial experiences.

Your wealth signature can range from riches to poverty and is created by every financial experience, belief, and thought you have been exposed to in this life and in other lives. Whatever financial situation you are experiencing, it is because that is what resonates with your wealth signature.

If your finances aren't where you'd like them to be, understanding your wealth signature will help you improve them. Start by asking yourself: How am I contributing to this lower money vibration? Try a structured self-exploration about money by answering these pertinent and clarifying questions:

- What are my earliest experiences with money?
- What are my beliefs surrounding money?
- What/who is influencing my beliefs on money?
- What money-related activities do I choose?
- Who am I spending time with – do they have poverty mindsets or abundant mindsets?

How do all of the above play into the money that I have, that I earn, that I spend, that I save, and that I invest? All of these things are related. When you begin to unfold the answers to these questions, your financial story will reveal itself. Once you understand the story, you can see what to work on, what to release, what to strengthen, and what to let blossom.

AN ABUNDANT MINDSET

The most important factor in having a high-vibrating wealth signature is to have an abundant mindset. The truth is, most of us have thoughts of abundance – just not as many as we want!

Take a moment to realize you already are magnetic to money. Your thoughts and emotions have brought exactly what you now possess in material items, money, and all forms of abundance. You are, indeed, an excellent manifester. But, now, it is time to manifest *even better*.

The first step in developing a more abundant

mindset is discovering why it is important to us that we have financial abundance. Often, when we want more money, it is symbolizing that we want more out of life. What this means is we are ready for growth and we are ready to tap further into our potential. However, how we translate that desire into reality is what shows the universe whether we are really ready for growth, or if we still need to re-work certain lessons.

Ask yourself: Why do you want increased financial abundance?

- Do you want fulfillment (a more fulfilling career, more life balance)?
- Do you want freedom (to travel, to pursue a passion)?
- Do you want to feel secure?
- Do you want to boost your self-esteem?
- Is your goal to release debt?
- Is your goal to "fix" the financial challenges you are experiencing?
- Is your goal to help others/make a difference?
- Is your goal simply to have more fun in life?

It's important for us to understand the why so we can begin to address the thought form that created a lack in the first place. For example, is your goal freedom? What "boxes" or parameters have you created in your mind to keep you from feeling free now? Are you seeking fulfillment? Money can make fulfillment seem easier in some ways, but your mindset can create this feeling with what you have right now. Do you seek more fun? What blocks have you created to having fun now?

When we say something like, "I want to have more money in order to feel secure and safe," what are we telling the universe? That we do *not* feel safe and secure. And that is a problem because if we don't feel safe and secure now, we won't feel that way no matter how much money we have. We have to cure the ailment, not just the symptom.

Once we understand where our desire for more abundance is rooted, we can shift that perception to bigger-picture thoughts. We can shift from "not having" to "having and wanting even more".

Financial abundance enables me to experience

> When we realize we are meant to bring light to the world, we can step back and visualize the bigger picture of how our empowered selves can spread that light.

even *more* fulfillment.

Financial abundance enables me to relish even *more* freedom.

Financial abundance enables me to enjoy even *more* security.

Financial abundance enables me to feel even *better* about myself.

Financial abundance enables me to experience even *more* independence.

Financial abundance enables me to live an even *simpler* life.

Financial abundance enables me to help even *more* people.

Financial abundance enables me to have even *more* fun.

When we have clarified our desires for abundance, then we return our focus to ourselves – the true source of our abundance.

YOU AS SOURCE

People tend to believe their financial abundance comes from somewhere else, and then when it doesn't come "enough", they blame it on that source. This is an excuse. External factors may provide a *means* of bringing abundance, but they are not the *source* of abundance. There is nothing and no one, anywhere or any time, that holds the power of your financial abundance – except for YOU. *We are the only ones who create, magnetize, receive, achieve, maintain, and grow our abundance.*

This, of course, brings us to the inherent question: What is your wealth signature?

- Do you vibrate at a survival level?
- Are you squeaking by, or living precipitously, month to month?
- Do you get your bills paid and have spending money?
- Do you get your bills paid and set aside small amounts as a backup?
- Do you have a generous living budget plus comfortable amounts on the side?
- Are you relatively well off with large assets or savings?
- Are you completely free financially, able to make all of your decisions based on preference rather than cost?

(Now, read that list again and notice how you feel lighter and lighter as you read. That gives you an idea of how raising your vibration feels in a physical sense.)

Once you are aware of where you are on the financial vibration scale, you can set a goal for where you want to be, understanding that you will step that way in increments as you adjust to each raise in vibration over time. It will be up to you to decide how far and how fast you will grow so drop your excuses. It's time for self-responsibility, self-creation, and self-mastery, leading to the abundant life you want.

LOVE AND MONEY

A discussion of our wealth signature and our ability to magnetize money is not complete without addressing self-love. A key to financial abundance, just like everything else in life, is love. We must love ourselves in order to feel worthy enough to receive abundance, maintain our wealth, and grow our financial resources. If there are parts of ourselves we don't love, our subconscious mind will find ways to create the financial difficulties we think we deserve. This separates us from the energy of money, rather than recognizing that it is part of our own energy.

We have to believe we deserve money. This can be tough, as we can find it easier to self-criticize than to self-praise at times. But when we realize we are meant to bring light to the world, we can step back and visualize the bigger picture of how our empowered selves can spread that light. When we set our sights on becoming a vessel designed for a higher purpose, it sets us free to soar with a wealth signature that is worthy of our soul's mission.

Principles of Abundance

Principle: All of us are capable of living in abundance.

Principle: Money is energy and, as such, is available to everyone in equal and infinite amounts.

Principle: Money is a tool that helps you live your intended life.

Principle: Because we live in a world that utilizes money, it is important for us to have "enough".

Principle: We expand our ability to create goodness when we have an abundance of money.

Important Ideas to Embrace True Abundance

Embrace the potential for cooperation and success for all.

Believe that all acts create goodness.

Follow your heart's joy.

Hone your ability to listen to and follow your intuition.

Master the balance of intention, action, and surrender.

Trust that everything that has happened, is happening, and will happen is for your highest and greatest good.

Know there is enough in the world.

The wealth within you, your essence, is your kingdom.
- Rumi

Universal Law of Compensation: Be easy to give and easy to receive in order to harness this Universal Law in regards to money, gifts, and abundance in all its forms, and keep your thoughts focused on the *value* your work brings.

Universal Law of Cause and Effect: You reap what you have sown with money and other forms of abundance. Keep your intentions clear and your intuition open to enjoy the fruits of your labor.

Creating Money: Keys to Abundance

by Sanaya Roman and Duane Packer

From Chapter 14: You Have What It Takes: A lot of you end up doing so many small tasks that you don't have time to create your life's work; you confuse busyness with accomplishing your higher purpose. You may have stacks of chores to be done and be rushing around, busy every moment. If you are going to get to your life's work, you need to take time to start it. Some of you say, "I'll do the important things after I finish all these errands, housework, paperwork, and so on." By the end of the day you may be too tired or have no time left.

Do those activities that take you closer to your life's work the first thing each day, or as soon as you possibly can. Spend five minutes thinking about your higher path as you wake up. Ask yourself, "Is there one action I could take today that would bring my life's work closer?" or "What is the most important action I could take today?" Make that your priority; do it before you do other things. It may be something as simple as energizing the symbol of your life's work, making a phone call, getting a book about a topic you are interested in, or setting up a space in your house to do a certain activity. You will be amazed at the way your life will change if the first thing you focus on and accomplish every day is something that will help make your dreams come true. Excerpt from *Creating Money* reprinted with permission. www.orindaben.com

Remember that all who succeed in life get off to a bad start, and pass through many heartbreaking struggles before they 'arrive.' The turning point in the lives of those who succeed usually comes at the moment of some crisis, through which they are introduced to their 'other selves.'

- Think and Grow Rich
by Napoleon Hill

Amplify
YOUR WHY

Call it conscious capitalism, or conscious leadership, or a conscious cause, but regardless of the output, Divas that Care Founder Candace Gish has found that passion is a primary uniting factor between women and their work. And it is that passion that she showcases through the Divas that Care movement, a multimedia platform for women to share their stories and receive the recognition she feels they deserve.

Originally created simply as a way for Gish to inspire her daughters, the platform has evolved to showcase passionate women and the potential they have to change their lives and impact others.

"I call these women the changemakers," said Gish.

"They are dynamic women who are really changing the face of the world. They are changing their families, and they are changing the communities around them."

She said she likes to feature women who "have drive and purpose, who step up to the plate, and who sometimes rock the boat."

"Women are powerful," said Gish. "Once we start to believe in ourselves and our purpose, we start projecting that belief, and this creates a catalyst ripple effect: when you affect that one person and then all these other things happen. I love connecting with women who have big goals and dreams and who want to make a difference."

One of the interesting factors she has discovered through interviewing women is that, however their actions manifest, there is always a deeper purpose, a deeper drive behind their actions. Whether it's to help their families or help a cause, women are motivated by a higher purpose. "They're doing these businesses because of something else," said Gish, and her goal is to connect these women to each other so that their respective missions can be amplified.

"As women, we are always searching – looking to improve and to develop," said Gish. "We search until we find a purpose, a higher purpose. And from there, we figure out who we are."

And it's that discovery of purpose that truly transforms lives, said Gish. "It brings more light into our bodies and our souls. It's this feeling of absolute happiness."

Gish believes we are hardwired to have more purpose. "I find that the people who are happier seem to have more purpose in their lives. Not just in business, but in life and causes or churches. When you are involved in more, you just feel better. You just do." She said when we find self-fulfillment, we have more drive and more love to give to others. "Our hearts have so much capacity to grow."

She said, "I really respect people who know who they are and want to share. They are

> Once we start to believe in ourselves and our purpose, we start projecting that belief, and this creates a catalyst ripple effect.

> As women, we are always searching – looking to improve and to develop. We search until we find a purpose, a higher purpose. And from there, we figure out who we are.

the changemakers. But sometimes they are misunderstood. Where other people are scared, I say, let's embrace them and love them. They just need somebody to be on their side. I really like the rocks that we can polish. I love people with beautiful souls, but I like those diamonds in the rough, too."

What she hopes women listeners and readers come away with — in addition to a sense of inspiration — is the knowledge that they are not alone. "Sometimes we don't find a support network inside our normal family and friends. Sometimes we need to look outside for that." And with Divas that Care, "There is somebody out there who has gone through something similar to them. There are dynamic individuals who are there for them."

She said, "I know what it's like to be by yourself, to feel like nobody understands what you are doing, to feel alone, to feel isolated. I think it's important for others not to feel that way. I want people to know we are there to support them. Business is not easy, life is not easy, there are turns and twists, good days and bad times. But there is something out there for each person. We celebrate each other's successes, but we're also relating to one another. Our platform is one that is only a positive place where we can support one another."

She said despite any of our differences, we are all on an evolving journey. "We learn every day, and we need to adjust things as we are learning for the next day. We are wired to evolve, and by looking at our own flaws, we actually are able to support others," she said. "How can we be of support to others if we are not willing to look at ourselves? We've got to always be doing something, learning something new."

She said it is "the best thing ever" to be able to run Divas that Care. "I think this is part of my life purpose, having this opportunity that I can do this for others, that I can support others. I absolutely love it. It brings a smile to my face every single day. My spirit is happy."

TIPS FOR STEPPING INTO YOUR PURPOSE

Collaborate with women who have similar goals and aspirations whenever possible

Actively seek out opportunities to assist, empower, and uplift others to form professional and personal sisterhoods

Approach your obstacles with an objective and positive mindset that supports your overall mission, vision, and company values

Candace Gish is the founder of the Divas that Care movement, an engaged community of women creating positive change in the world and sharing their experiences as a way to support and uplift each other. Is your passion to create positive change in the world? Listen to the Divas that Care Podcast or apply to be a guest at www.divasthatcare.com.

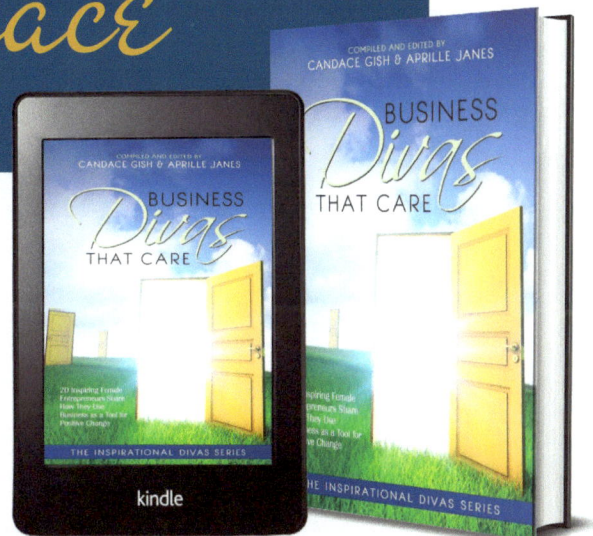

Swirls of Color

A Real-Life Story of Creating a New Course

If that can't work, or if they won't let me play with them, then how do I keep fighting for my dream?

Courtney Joyner thought fate was a nice concept — in theory at least — but it wasn't until a chance stop at a Colorado pottery studio that she realized the power of following a path of passion.

In one moment, her shiny, previously desired corporate path paled in comparison to the pursuit of art and entrepreneurship. And just like that, she formed Brush Strokes Pottery, a mobile, paint-your-own-pottery studio and webstore based in Austin, Texas.

Of course, as all entrepreneurs learn, "just like that" was not so simple.

"In the beginning, I made so many plans, followed all the rules — only to face disappointment and closed doors," she said. But rather than discourage her, those moments fueled her. "They allowed me to self-reflect and ask myself, what was it I was truly desiring? Did I want something everyone else was doing or something unique that takes bravery?"

She said each and every time there were closed doors or opportunities, "I picked myself back up, dusted myself off, and said, 'Well, what's next?' If that can't work, or if they won't let me play with them, then how do I keep fighting for my dream?"

The universe sent me a wakeup call and said, "There is more in store for you — go get it!"

Joyner was taught early in life that when someone throws you a curveball, you shake it off and keep playing. "Literally that exact thing happened to me playing tee ball as a child. A line drive ball nailed me in the shin, and I started crying. I have a vivid memory of my dad telling me to shake it off and keep playing. Some might think that's too much tough love, but I'm thankful for the life lessons it taught me. Life is always going to throw you curveballs. Sometimes you may duck and get out of the line of fire, and sometimes you may get hit. It's when that ball hits that you have an opportunity — an opportunity to make a choice to move forward with strength or to cower with fear. It's those life situations that help develop your character and strengthen your drive."

But little did she know that the discovery of her passion was not enough. Not long after starting Brush Strokes Pottery, life threw another curveball, and she was rocked by personal tragedy. Suddenly, every part of her life faced enormous challenges.

"I had no idea why this was happening," she said. "There were so many unanswered questions I had because I felt like life had been working out great. WRONG! Little did I know I was stuck in a rut and couldn't even see it. The universe sent me a wakeup call and said, 'There is more in store for you — go get it!'"

Forced temporarily to return to the corporate world, "I knew that I would find a way back to being an entrepreneur one way or another, but I didn't know how. I held faith that whatever God and the Universe had in store for me would come to me in due time. Let me tell you, patience is not a virtue of mine so that was tough. But I did a great deal of soul searching and a little floundering, and ultimately the wait was worth it."

The space from her business showed her a bigger picture that she had been missing: that her mission was to serve her customers *and* her soul.

"Throughout my life, I've had a knack for bringing people together and making them feel at ease. People have always told me they feel comfortable around me and that they could tell me anything. And at every single pottery or painting event I have hosted, people comment on the therapeutic nature they feel when painting. For a moment, they forget about their daily stresses and are simply present in life. The smiles I see on their faces, the laughter as friends joke and brainstorm … it's infectious. Knowing that I bring people together to feel that sense of joy absolutely 100 percent feeds

my soul."

She said with the re-incarnation of Brush Strokes today, "I've melded two talents together, like swirls of color, to create something that is bigger than a job to me — it's what I feel like I was called to do."

She said, "If you'd asked me 20 years ago where I'd be in life, this is not where I would have thought! But sometimes the off-beaten path can bring you the fullest joy. There are days [even now] where honestly I'm not sure what I'm doing and I'm at a loss, figuring things out on the fly. There are days where everything goes wrong and I question. But I know deep down this is what feeds my soul so I hold faith that everything happens for a reason and what's in store for me is coming in its own way."

One of Joyner's favorite quotes is, "Even if you fall, you're still moving forward." Her advice to passionate entrepreneurs? Pick up your feet and move!

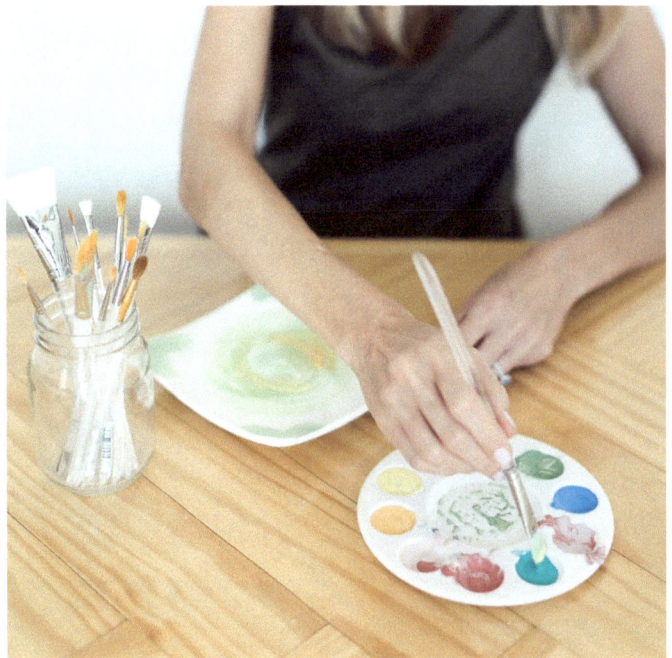

JOYNER'S ADVICE FOR ENTREPRENEURIAL CONNECTING

Resonating with Authenticity

Today, people are resonating with honesty. They want to see real, raw emotions from celebrities, politicians, companies, and individuals. People support and want to buy from people they feel they know.

Whatever your goals are in life — whether you are seeking a job in the corporate sector or you want to be your own boss — Joyner says it's important to remember who you are and keep with that honesty and integrity. She says that's what sets you apart and that's why people will be drawn to you.

For example, Joyner utilizes her pottery to spread happiness, so not only are her products joyful but so is her approach. "Brush Strokes is all about bringing people joy. Whether they can de-stress from their life while painting or feel joy when giving a custom gift, I want people to feel happy — so that's what I give. By being open and honest with myself and others, I have created a community that supports my business year after year."

Courtney Joyner is the founder of Brush Strokes Pottery, a mobile, paint-your-own-pottery studio in Austin, Texas. Visit www.brushstrokespottery.com for upcoming events and pre-made pottery in the webstore.

Enchanted
Makeovers

Before ...

After ...

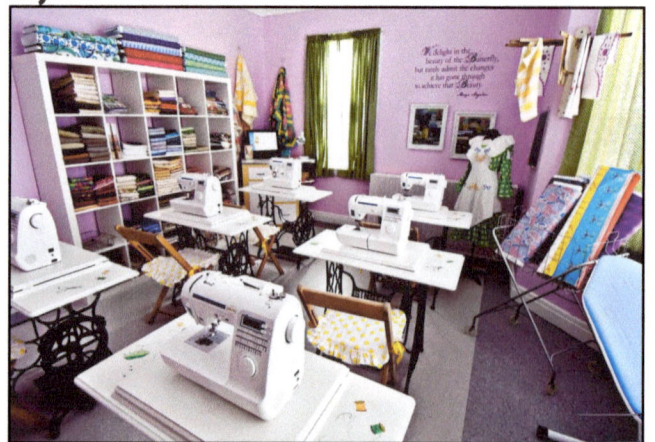

How could the women and children in the shelter realize that they were worthy of so much more? They, too, had dreams, but where could they be found again?

A Sacred Journey to Transform Lives

In 2007, Terry Grahl found herself looking at a path to nowhere. Standing on a chipped staircase in a dark hallway, she was overwhelmed with a sense of despair. She had been asked to volunteer her time painting a wall at a women's shelter, but what she found in the stark dorm-style building was not just a bare wall but stained mattresses, walls held together by duct tape, prison-style bunk beds, and throwaway blankets worn threadbare and dull.

As she immersed herself in the bleak surroundings, Terry envisioned what the women and children living there felt every day: crushing reminders of lost hopes and dreams, flashbacks of pain and heartbreak, and a reflection of all that was blocking them in life. What stared back at her were not open doors to the creation of happy, fulfilling, joy-filled lives. What stared back at her was an omnipresent sense of unworthiness and hopelessness.

How could this be ok?

Handmade is Heart-made

Terry had grown up believing that handmade meant from the heart, that nurturing the soul was as necessary as nurturing the body. How could these families heal in an environment that felt more like punishment than opportunity? How could the women and children in the shelter realize that they were worthy of so much more? They, too, had dreams, but where could they be found again?

A Moment that Changed Everything

As the owner of a new interior design service, Terry had talent and skill, but as she stared at the enormity of it all, she asked, "Why am I here, and how could I possibly do all of this?"

Enter fate. Enter God. Enter destiny. Enter an understanding that whatever is meant to happen will happen because from that one moment, everything changed.

The Birth of Enchanted Makeovers

What started with Terry's tentative offer to help paint one wall blossomed into a national program of healing and hope and nurturing and love. By transforming shelters, Enchanted Makeovers has provided a new perspective on life to tens of thousands of women, children, and female veterans in shelters, many of whom have experienced human trafficking, post-traumatic stress disorder, sexual

ENCHANTED MAKEOVERS
Leadership Team Member Sunshine Windsor Clark
& Founder Terry Grahl

abuse, and domestic violence.

Today, Enchanted Makeovers has grown even further with programs that help women and children embrace creativity, practice mindfulness, revel in self-expression, and develop their self-worth. One of these programs is Sacred Sewing Room, which dedicates a sacred space at shelters for the learning of an artistic skill that translates into personal fulfillment, a means to provide comfort in a new home, and, in some cases, even income.

Enchanted Makeovers also has volunteers all over the country who craft handmade pillowcases, handmade dolls, and even handmade superhero capes to help children entering the shelters believe they can be the heroes of their own lives.

To learn more, visit www.enchantedmakeovers. org.

"In 2008, my daughter and I came to Grace Centers of Hope in search of a new life. I had been struggling with an addiction to prescription pills and was running away from an abusive marriage. At one of the darkest points in my life, God crossed my path with Terry's. Her servitude was symbolic to my own personal pursuit at that point in time. We watched a metamorphosis take place in our surroundings as we were simultaneously experiencing the freedom from our former lives. Her visions inspire optimism, comfort, encouragement, and reassurance. It is truly an honor to now have the opportunity to give back to an organization that is dear to my heart and to work alongside many amazing women that I deeply admire."
- Sunshine Windsor Clark

SOCKS = LOVE

How two women discovered that sharing socks is sharing love

On the Tuesday night before Thanksgiving in 2011, Sue Lee was shopping for the holiday dinner, deep in thought about her arriving guests, how much food she should buy, and what she still needed to clean at home. The last thing she expected was to receive a message from God in the grocery store.

But, there it was. Like a marquee sign in her head, in yellow block letters with a red outline: SOCK IT TO EM CAMPAIGN SOCKS FOR THE HOMELESS.

Stunned, she thought, "Really, God, you want me to do what?"

Lee didn't know anything about the homeless. And this certainly was not the best timing. She pushed her cart faster through the store, hoping she could "out shop" the words. But the message kept running through her mind's eye. Try as she might, the message was received, and like many great missions in life, it began with a small step.

"You won't believe what just happened …!" she shared with her good friend Phillis Shimamoto. Lee also emailed a few girlfriends: "I've got an idea. Let's collect socks from Thanksgiving to the end of December and then take them to a shelter!"

Lee and her friends collected 575 pair of socks. Happy with the results, they arrived at the Denver Rescue Mission to deliver them on a seven-degree

day. As soon as they opened the hatch of their car, they were crowded by people walking up to them. "Socks! You have socks? Can we have a pair?" they asked.

"They were wearing tattered coats, ill-fitting shoes, worn-out hats, no gloves … We were shocked. They began thanking us and told us that socks meant even more than food. I cry still to think of it," said Lee.

Lee and Shimamoto looked at each other in that moment and knew they had to do more.

They learned that socks were the most needed item at shelters, yet the least donated. They learned that as many as two-thirds of the homeless suffer from foot problems. They learned there are thousands of men, women, and children who go without socks on a daily basis.

They were heartbroken. And also filled with resolve to put new socks on as many feet in the United States that needed them. Reaching out to everyone they knew, they asked them to be what Shimamoto branded as "Sock Ambassadors," people who collect socks whenever they want, from whoever they want, for as long as they want.

It worked. That new season, Lee and Shimamoto picked up socks from those in the Denver Metro

> **Receiving a pair of socks is like getting a hug, along with a message that your life matters and that someone is thinking about you.**

Sock it to Em Founders Sue Lee and Phillis Shimamoto

area. They counted and sorted and took them to shelters and other places that serve citizens experiencing homelessness. Out-of-state Sock Ambassadors collected, sorted, and bagged their own socks for their local areas. When the season ended, Lee and Shimamoto stared at the numbers. They had organized the collection of 10,000 pair of socks.

Yet, that's when the magic really started. Friends told friends, agencies and shelters started calling. Several churches declared No Socks Sundays, where congregants attended church not wearing socks and, instead, brought a pair to donate. In 2014, several mayors declared a similarly themed work day. The Denver Police Department and the Denver Sheriff's Department battled it out to see who could collect the most socks. (Denver Police won twice.) Offices and event organizers shared peanut butter and jelly sandwiches and socks. By 2015, Lee and Shimamoto, along with their healthy support group, had delivered 78,264 pairs of socks. By 2018, it was hundreds of thousands.

Lee and Shimamoto have learned the act of sharing socks is so much more than a physical act. "For those who are experiencing homelessness, socks equal love," said Lee. "Receiving a pair of socks is like getting a hug, along with a message that your life matters and that someone is thinking about you."

By that measure, Lee and Shimamoto and all of the Sock It To Em supporters have given out lots of hugs and lots of messages of love. Oh, and lots of socks.

Takeaway
It doesn't take more than a spark of desire to create an impact. Relying almost exclusively on donations and volunteer labor, Sock It To Em has added over $1 million of goodness into the nationwide community!

The youngest Sock Ambassador, four-year-old Bryce Valentine, watched his older sister collect socks for her elementary school classes. Patiently waiting until he entered preschool, he said, "I get to be a Sock Ambassador now, right Mom?"

Regina Schroeder, the first out-of-state Sock Ambassador, has provided socks to every school in Manhattan, Kansas. Here, with KSU's Theta Xi.

Become a Sock It To Em Ambassador!
Collect socks from friends, family, co-workers, and neighbors! Make a social impact one pair of socks at a time and discover how Socks = Love! Learn more at sockittoemsockcampaign.org

Often we view love as a "search". We believe we have to go somewhere, do something, be a certain way to find love.

If we're lucky, what we discover on the external search is that love is inside of us and always has been inside of us. The journey takes us on a path toward our own hearts, where the greatest treasure imaginable resides.

Evey fiber of our being, down to the smallest particle, is love. We have love. We are love. We provide love for the entire universe, simply by existing.

Adapted from *Love Like God: Embracing Unconditional Love*

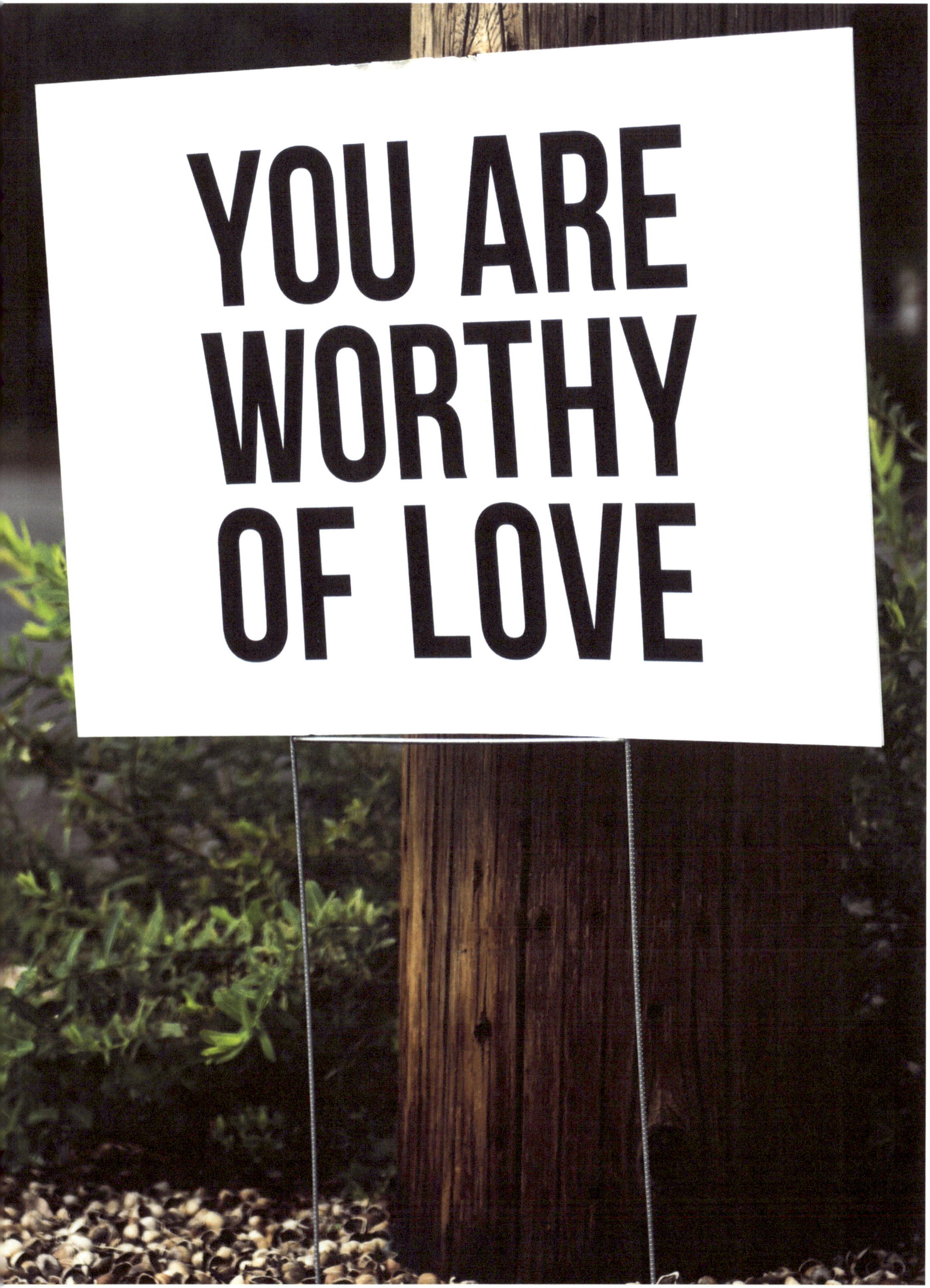
YOU ARE
WORTHY
OF LOVE

Healing
with
ANIMALS

KATE NELIGAN

The first time I witnessed equine-assisted therapy and coaching, I was in awe. I watched a group of recovering addicts transform from disconnected and distraught to happy, grounded, and hopeful — in less than two hours. From that moment, I understood in a clear way that the human-animal bond is life-changing.

I had loved animals my entire life and considered them friends and family, but I hadn't realized they also were healers and teachers. Horses, in particular, seem to be powerful healers primed to read our emotional states, reflect our truths, reveal the stories we tell ourselves, and help us with our core wounds.

Winston Churchill said, "There is something about the outside of a horse that is good for the inside of a man." (Of course, that holds true for women and children, too). He was able to give voice to the phenomenon that I now witness every week with my clients — people change for the better in the presence of a horse's unconditional love and from being outside in nature.

While digital technology brings us rapid connection, horses show us the meaning of authentic, heartfelt,

slow, and meaningful connection. Horses teach what "power within" means, rather than the dynamic of "power over". I've even found that horses help us become better leaders, as they only follow when we get intentional, clear, and kind in our communication.

Through work with horses, we can learn an entirely new way of being, one that connects us more to ourselves, each other, and the world. This type of therapy allows people to experience oneness in a hands-on way that creates breakthroughs in all areas of their lives.

Of course, horses aren't the only ones that can help us become our best selves. As humans, we feel connected with a wide variety of animals. The most-viewed viral videos tend to be beautiful stories of the human-animal bond, illustrated by humans and birds, donkeys, lions, and many more species. Cat cafes have cropped up to offer cuddle time with feline friends, and goat yoga is now a popular new athletic activity. Animals also are becoming increasingly incorporated into meditation and play therapy.

While the philosophy that being around furry creatures helps our mood makes common sense, there is actually science behind the idea as well. HABRI (Human-Animal Bond Research Institute) has done studies that show human-animal bonding fosters improvements in several areas:

Physical health: greater relaxation, lowered blood pressure, increased physical activity, and more

Mental health: reductions in anxiety, stress, depression, and loneliness; and enhancements in well-being and social support

Emotional health: greater life satisfaction, quality of life, belief in life purpose/meaning, and levels of trust

Photo credits:
Michelle Tritten (goat, above)
Chuck Rockford (horse, left)

Animals offer us the opportunity to become present and play with them, walk them for exercise, and drop into our hearts as we touch them. They remind us to just be!

This is proof that being with animals is truly medicinal. That word "being" is key, though. Animals offer us the opportunity to become present and play with them, walk them for exercise, and drop into our hearts as we touch them. They remind us to just be! To reap the full benefits of the connectedness we experience around them, we must set aside the chaos that often surrounds our responsibilities and "doing-based" lives. We must remember to take the journey back into our bodies and slow down enough to fully live and love the moment.

Of course, we can do this with our own animals, or we can volunteer. We also can utilize equine-assisted learning with a coach or as part of a group workshop or corporate team-building exercise. Regardless of the method, seeing ourselves reflected in animals is powerful.

My personal wish is for us all to walk in the world seeing our animal partners for who they truly are: the best reminders of unconditional love and presence on the planet. So, the next time you see friendly critters, remember to pause and thank them for the benefits they bring humanity.

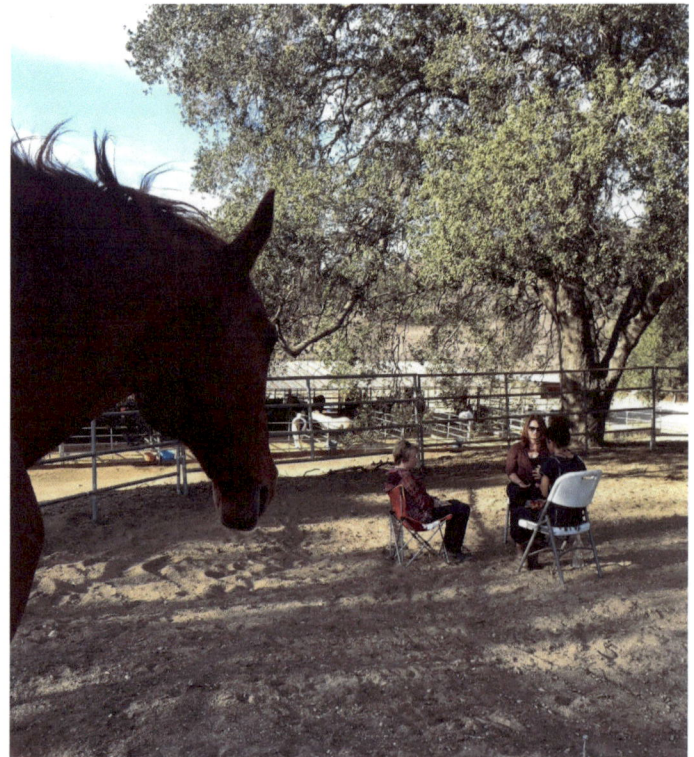

Kate Neligan has a Master of Spiritual Psychology and is an equine-assisted life and career coach who conducts group workshops, corporate team building and leadership trainings, and private consultations for clients all over the United States. Visit www.consciousrockstar.com for event dates and locations and to inquire about services.

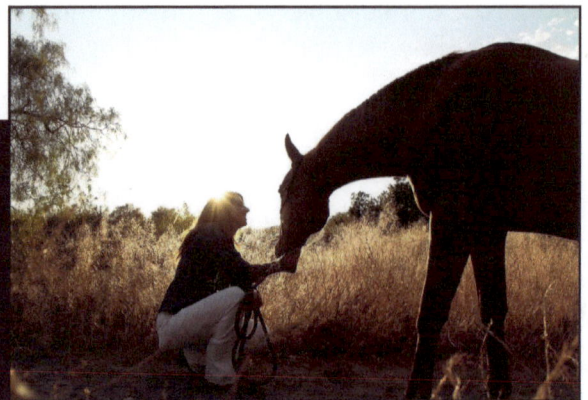

*As you start
to walk on the
way, the way
appears.*

– Rumi

Divine Timing:
A Soul Mate's Journey

Nicole Kovalcik

A few years ago, the Law of Attraction seemed to be everywhere all at once. I saw books and magazines on the subject, plus movies and a TV show. If it had been in the world of fashion, the Law of Attraction would have been the new "It" bag of the season.

I admit, I was intrigued. What a concept: If you put positive energy into the universe, you'll get it back! If you think it, it will come. It sounded simple enough. Why not try it? Little did I know that the Law of Attraction would change life as I knew it ...

My 42nd birthday was quickly approaching, and I faced a serious reckoning in my life. Due to a merger, my company was letting me go after 21 years. I'd never married or had children. Instead, I had buried myself in my career to distract me from the fact that I was living a solitary

life. Suddenly, with no career to hide behind, I knew the life I had was not enough.

I picked myself up from my thoughts and went down to the Jersey shore. It had always been my sacred place, but that day it was more. As I stared at the ocean, the water filled me with a sense of peace and the determination to figure out what I truly wanted for my life using the Law of Attraction.

I started a gratitude journal. The more I journaled and purged, the more at peace and calm I felt. I went through my condo and donated whatever hadn't been used in the last year. I also stopped hanging onto things, especially those with bad memories attached to them. I knew I needed to make space for the good things I didn't know were on the horizon.

I made peace with my past

and focused on what I wanted. I wrote a list of goals that came from the deepest, best place in me — not from fear or ego. It started with, "I will weigh xxx and pay off my credit cards by a certain date," then, "I will see my friends at least once a month," but it was number six that I gave the heaviest thought ... my ideal partner.

Even with my upcoming employment changes looming, I knew I would be okay. Financially it might be a bit rocky, but I'd figure that out. Even with no one to share my life with, I was okay. I'd always be okay, but was "okay" what I truly wanted? It wasn't. I wanted a partner.

After much soul searching, I wrote, "I will be in a loving relationship with a slightly older man, who is open, honest, secure in employment; who likes to have fun, lots of sex, watch

I finished my list, turned the page, and left it for the universe. That's when everything changed.

football, play sports (tennis/golf), go to the beach, spend time with family and friends; and who loves me for me — when I'm quiet or loud, happy or sad, sick or healthy." If I was meant to be with someone, that was who I wanted. I finished my list, turned the page, and left it for the universe.

That's when everything changed.

Nearly three weeks later, as I wished my cousin "Happy Birthday" on Facebook, I saw a familiar face with the post, "Looking for some answers but I am not finding any. Is this supposed to be a test in life? … Just don't know and I'm tired." His name was Kenny, better known as "K2".

K2 had been co-captain, along with my high school boyfriend, of our football team. Two months earlier, he had popped up as "someone I might know" so I friend-requested him and he accepted. K2 had been a carefree senior with a quirky laugh and the bluest eyes. He'd headed to the U.S. Merchant Marine Academy after high school to become a deck officer, which was a big deal. And something in his post stuck with me.

I finally did something I never did — I commented. "I know just how that is. Hang in there." For 16 hours, we messaged stories of our lives, and while we hadn't really been friends in high school, it felt like we had known each other forever.

After a few days of messaging, he mentioned he was coming up from South Carolina for a Giants vs. Redskins football game and offered to buy me a ticket. I froze. This guy I knew in high school — who I had reconnected with for a few days — wanted to drive 12 hours to take me to a football game. Was I crazy to go?

I hemmed and hawed, even polled my friends about it. This was way outside of my comfort zone! Ultimately, I figured, we'd go to the game, become friends, and probably never see each other again, right?

My fingers typed, "I'm in."

When game day arrived, he drove through the night, while I made tons of breakfast food and chicken parmigiana with lasagna for dinner. I bought Guinness and made sandwiches for tailgating. I was a wreck.

I heard his flip-flops as he neared my door. I went out to greet him, and it was like I was hit by a two-by-four.

That moment, my life changed.

We went to the game and ended up parking two rows from my brother. What were the odds? Like everything with us, it just flowed. K2 gave me my last first kiss in the parking lot of the Giants stadium, and in the wee hours of the morning, he proposed.

It wasn't the usual on-bended-knee proposal.

He said, "When the ink dries on my divorce papers, marry me."

Without hesitation, I replied, "YES."

I offered to buy him a plane ticket to come back the next weekend, but he was headed out to sea soon and wanted to spend time with his kids, so he couldn't. *Was it a sign?* I wondered. I grabbed a photo of my grandparents holding me on my christening day and said, "If I'm not supposed to be with K2, let loose every obstacle and stop this now. Otherwise, find a way for us be together." I closed my eyes and took a breath.

An hour later, K2 messaged that he would see me that Friday afternoon. In that moment, I knew we were meant to be.

Hurricane Sandy turned what would have been a four-day weekend into a special eight. And, then, he left for sea, and our life became phone calls, texts, and emails. K2 came back to Jersey for the Super Bowl and met my entire family, and then we went to South Carolina to look at houses, even though we hadn't decided where to live. As we walked through a model home, I envisioned us living there. He squeezed my hand, and I knew. I looked into his eyes and said, "I want this. I want to buy this house."

While the home was being built, I lived with his parents. Three days after it closed, I was let go from my job. Five months later, his divorce was finalized, and he got a call that his ship was delayed out another day due to fog. He asked if I wanted to get married that night. I said, "I'm in."

Our friends, Jim and Sandie, performed the ceremony in our new home. K2's proposal had been spot-on: He divorced at noon, and we married 10 hours

I'd been in just the right place to get out of my own way.

later. It wasn't planned to be that way, but the opportunity presented itself and we took it.

It wasn't until a year later that I realized K2 ticked off every point listed in number six of my goals list and that the universe literally had delivered him to my front door. I'd been in just the right place to get out of my own way. I had been open to change, surrendered, and then dove in. I realize now that all of our life experiences had prepared us to be ready for each other.

The timing was everything. What if I wasn't being let go from my job? What if I hadn't remembered him? What if my cousin's birthday wasn't that day — she was the reason I joined Facebook to begin with — would I even have seen his post? What if the Giants weren't playing the Skins? Any one of those things could've changed everything.

I see now that there was a divine plan, and it had to unfold in its own time.

I see now that there was a divine plan, and it had to unfold in its own time. We met for the first time in 1984, and it took 28 years for us to reconnect. Now, we're celebrating the rest of our lives together. It took us a long time to get here, but we're here now and it was worth every moment of preparation. If I had to go through all of it again to get here, I'd do it!

I know now that if we look deep within ourselves and are honest with how we want life to be, we can make it happen. It may not happen overnight, but if we practice gratitude and surrender, good things will happen. I'm proof positive of it.

Make the Law of Attraction *work for you ...*

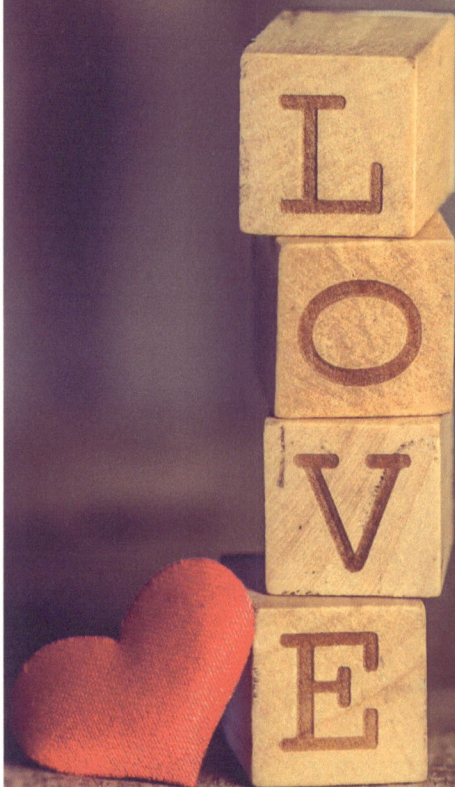

1. Dig deep and make a list of what you really, really, really want. Then, let it go.

2. Clear the clutter, including digital clutter, especially if it makes you feel sad or hurt.

3. Get out of your own way, and relinquish control ... It's not easy, but it's a must!

4. Step away from your comfort zone, and go with your gut. It won't steer you wrong.

5. Know that there's a plan far bigger than yours, just waiting to show itself to you.

6. Practice gratitude for what you have now and all that's coming your way.

Nicole Kovalcik
After 21 years in various roles within the PBM industry, I was given an offer I couldn't refuse. With that, I made a few major life changes. Now, my focus is being the best wife and doggie mama and writing two blogs that are a labor of love: www.stillafloatnk2.wordpress.com and www.beingabullymama.wordpress.com.

From *Spiritual Growth: Being Your Higher Self* by Sanaya Roman

Trust that what other people do will in some way be for your higher good, even if you don't understand why. No matter what happens, tell yourself the universe is perfect, and everything that happens is perfect. If something you were hoping for doesn't happen, know that something even better will. Don't try to force your Higher Self to create your pictures on how things ought to be; know that a higher wisdom is always operating. Remember that your Higher Self is always giving you as much good as you will allow into your life.

Deepen Your Relationship
through GRATITUDE

Sarah Hackley

When I was growing up, my family experienced more than its fair share of loss and tragedy. And those experiences broke many of the relationships around me. The few that lasted, however, were the ones in which the partners continually turned to each other for support and encouragement while simultaneously showing how valued that support was. Those were the relationships in which the partners never took each other for granted, and those were the ones that remained intact.

I kept those lessons in mind throughout my adolescence and early adulthood, and I took them with me into my marriage. From day one, I was determined to never take my husband for granted. To never let the many little things he does each day go unnoticed. To always maintain that little-something-extra so often associated only with new relationships. And that effort has rewarded me in unexpected ways.

About six months after my husband and I married, I came down with viral meningitis and I never completely recovered. While I was up and out of bed about a month later, I started experiencing a multitude of new symptoms that culminated a year later into an autoimmune diagnosis.

When my husband and I met, I had been living

THINGS I LOVE ABOUT YOU

> **While I'm an inherently optimistic person, I know that my optimism isn't what's pulling me past — and sometimes through — that darkness. It's gratitude.**

with chronic migraine for more than a decade. So I was no stranger to pain, medications, limitations, or adapting to challenges. But this new illness is different, and treating it (particularly without exacerbating the migraine) has proven to be especially difficult.

There are times when those difficulties threaten to take me to a dark place. And while I'm an inherently optimistic person, I know that my optimism isn't what's pulling me past — and sometimes through — that darkness. It's gratitude.

Gratitude is a powerful emotion, and its expression has a bidirectional influence on both our minds and our relationships. When we feel gratitude, we also feel contentment and satisfaction. We believe we have — and are — enough. And those feelings and beliefs generate positive vibrations that bring us even more of what we appreciate.

When we express gratitude, we focus on the things, qualities, and events that bring us joy and happiness, and we bask in those feelings. As we continue to express gratitude and focus on what we appreciate, we train our minds to see less of what we don't. That positive mindset opens us up to appreciate more and more of what's around us, which opens us up to receiving even more.

Expressing gratitude also lifts up our partners. Showing them they are appreciated fills them with contentment and satisfaction, just as feeling grateful does for us. It is a positive reminder that they are more than enough. Our expression of gratitude also lets them know they are loving us in the ways we need, whether that's through physical touch, words of affirmation, acts of service, gifts, quality time, or a combination of these love languages. This knowledge generates a positive desire to go above and beyond — to love even harder.

These effects are why gratitude and its expression are vital to healthy relationships. Gratitude creates strong, positive bonds. And it helps maintain those bonds even through difficult times.

We can't feel immensely grateful for one aspect of our lives while despairing over another. On my darkest days, in my darkest moments, I need only think of my husband and I'm already smiling, heading back toward the light. In those moments, gratitude reminds me: I have everything I ever dreamed.

For I *am* grateful. So completely, eternally grateful

for the marriage with which I've been blessed and for the man I get to call "husband". And I continue to express that gratitude — with love notes, silly kiss emojis, treats, chores, "I love you"s, and "thank you"s — every single day. In return, my husband, who is regularly reminded of how much he is appreciated, consistently goes out of his way to love me harder, which only makes me more grateful. And so the cycle continues.

CULTIVATING GRATITUDE

When was the last time you expressed appreciation for your partner? Left a love note? Brought home a favorite treat? Said, "Thank you"? If it's been longer than 24 hours, I encourage you to seek out ways to express that appreciation today.

Feeling and expressing gratitude is one of those things that is easier the more you do it. If you're struggling to feel gratitude or show your partner appreciation, try:

- Reading a book on love languages and figuring out which one speaks best to your partner.
- Making a daily practice of sharing the one or two best parts of your day.
- Keeping a gratitude journal.
- Saying "thank you" for the small things.
- Asking your partner what thing you might do to be a better partner to him/her.
- Texting, emailing, or IMing your partner to share one thing you especially appreciate about them or to simply say you are appreciative (s)he is in your life.

Sarah Hackley is the editor for Absolute Love Publishing and the author of *Finding Happiness with Migraines: A Do It Yourself Guide*, *Preparing to Fly: Financial Freedom from Domestic Abuse*, and *The Things We Lose*. She also is a patient advocate, writing and wellness coach, and poet. Learn more at www.sarahhackley.com.

EVERYDAY TIPS to
Consciously Create

a Life You Love

Denise Thompson

Anyone who genuinely and consistently with both hands looks for something, will find it. - Rumi

Recognize how important and healing sleep is. Give yourself permission to leave non-essential things undone in order to make time for a nap or to get to bed early. Perhaps even try a sleep mask, as there is a release in shutting out all physical light. Allow yourself the gift of rejuvenating rest.

Tell yourself good morning! Instead of rolling out of bed and thinking about all your tasks for the day, take 30 seconds to welcome the fresh start and wish for a smooth and positive day. While you're in bed, morning-stretch your arms and legs to get "in" your body, ready to face the day present and aware.

Boost your daily hydration intake. During the daily hubbub, it is easy to forego the liquid love our bodies crave. Try to add more quality water and nourishing beverages to the busiest part of your day. Consider making a pitcher of water the night before with natural flavors (such as strawberries and basil, rosemary and citrus, or cucumber and mint) so it is ready for your to-go container in the morning!

Choose one area of your room or home that is stagnant and energize it. Going through the motions of our normal routine can make us blind to how things can get stuck. A change can be as small as cleaning out and rearranging a sock drawer so you can easily find and grab the right cozy pair or decluttering that one kitchen junk drawer where you can never find what you need, or the change can be as big as re-arranging furniture. Changing things up can provide ease in functionality, a positive emotional energizing, and an opportunity to see things in a new light.

Listen to favorite songs from your life's soundtrack. There is nothing like music that evokes strong emotional and physical reactions from your body and soul. Choosing music from your life's most exciting, cherished, and milestone moments and memories will bring that energy and upbeat feeling

instantly back. And since music is so portable, create your own "mixtape playlist" for driving in the car, working on the computer, cleaning up the house, weeding your garden, working out, or while doing other physical pursuits. Let the power of music put some pep in your step!

Find one thing today where you can let go of your pursuit for perfection. Embrace the qualities and quirks of your mind and body, and realize we are all perfectly imperfect as we are. Appreciating your favorite attributes, inherited qualities, and emotional strengths will leave no time for negative self-talk.

Allow yourself to catch a curveball with patience and grace. You are meant to experience life in all its glorious forms, which includes love, joy, sadness, uncertainty, happiness, forgiveness, and challenges. While we can sometimes influence the process, move forward with the peace of knowing the outcome will be as it is meant to be for your emotional and spiritual growth.

In a moment where you might normally contract, catch yourself. Instead, change course and open your whole heart. Every loving encounter enriches us and the other person. Allow your loving cup to overflow.

Do something nice. Express your gratitude for life by choosing acts of service. Giving your time and presence of mind is a priceless gift not only to others, but to yourself as well. Whether it's for a family member, neighbor, or co-worker or volunteering for others, feeling we have helped someone is its own reward.

Take a moment in nature. Go on a walk, stand outside while you're on the phone, take five minutes to nap on the porch. Let the good vibes sink into your body and help you have a better day!

I know you're tired, but, come, this is the way. - Rumi

HALOTHERAPY

USE SALT TO HEAL YOUR BODY

Dating back hundreds of years, halotherapy is a natural health treatment that utilizes the antibacterial and antimicrobial properties of salt. The treatment can take various forms, including a salt bath, a saltwater gargle, or even a visit to the beach, but recently this ancient treatment is popping up in the United States in a new way: centers that enable patrons to breathe in and sit in heavily salted air. The idea is that, through the natural processes of breathing and exposure, the salt reaches airways and helps to thin and expel mucous, while also resting on the skin and enabling healing of skin conditions.

The Salt Therapy Association says this treatment can relieve ailments such as asthma, allergies, bronchitis, chronic obstructive pulmonary disease, colds, cystic fibrosis, ear infections, and sinusitis, as well as skin conditions like acne, eczema, psoriasis, rashes, and rosacea.

While this treatment is relatively new in the United States, Austin Salt Cave Owner Jack Cramer said it has been used around the world for centuries. More than 200 years ago in Poland, for example, doctors discovered that salt miners were healthier than other miners and

the general public. This led to the creation of breathing clinics located in the salt mines. Today, he said, European doctors prescribe visits to salt rooms for illnesses and ailments related to the lungs, as salt can help heal the areas it can "physically get to and touch", including the "nooks and crannies of your sinuses and lungs".

The Austin Salt Cave in Austin, Texas, utilizes an ultra-fine salt mist dispersed into a cave-like room filled with 11 tons of pink Himalayan salt, including salt boulders, a dozen extra-tall salt lamps, a salt tile wall, and even salt on the floor, which Cramer said pulls toxins from the pores of the feet and "feels like a foot massage, kind of like walking on a beach but more coarse". The combined effect is a peaceful amber glow, much like stepping into an actual Himalayan salt lamp.

"Pink Himalayan salt is just so beautiful," said Cramer "It has an amazing color of pink or a pink-orange glow. There's something about it that is just so different, so relaxing."

In his facility, while the ambiance reflects Himalayan pink salt, it is pharmacy-grade sodium chloride that is pumped into the air in what he describes as a "modern interpretation of a Polish salt mine". He said there are some benefits to using Himalayan pink salt and some to using pharmacy-grade salt, but notably, "Each salt deposit is different with minerals and elements, and some you may not want to breathe in. To eliminate that variable, we use that pure, pure salt. It's supposed to provide the best effect because it is just salt. It's nice, clean, and sterile so you can heal."

Cramer, who has experienced asthma since age six, said, "If you're not breathing at 100 percent, you're not functioning at 100 percent. That stress and fear and uncertainty of not being able to breathe – I want to do anything I can do to help other people alleviate that."

Frequent clients of the Austin Salt Cave are people looking to improve their severe breathing conditions, but Cramer said the therapy is also good for healthier and clearer skin, a healthy respiratory tract in general, and for athletes looking for that extra edge. "Plus, I have a lot of people who use it as a chance to decompress. They can lock the phone awhile, take a nap, or get away from the kids for a while."

There are only about 100 facilities in the entire U.S., so the Austin Salt Cave has an active clientele. In addition to the breathing room services, Cramer rents the room out for yoga classes, meditations, and breathing classes.

"Pranayama yoga breathing is awesome," he said. "It pairs so well with salt." Cramer even hosts a local woman's singing bowl concerts. He said that during the sessions, "You can feel the sound vibration through the whole body."

For those interested in natural health options, halotherapy looks to be a positive way to tap into the body's healing ability. Are you interested in the healing effects of halotherapy? For more information or to take a look at available products, visit austinsaltcave. com or search online for a facility in your area.

WHAT TO EXPECT

Dress comfortably, as you'll likely be reclining.

If looking for an improvement in your skin, expose as much as is appropriate.

You likely will taste salt on your lips, but you will not leave covered in visible salt.

Plan to leave all electronics outside the room, both for relaxation and because the fine salt mist can damage electronics.

As salt attracts moisture, be sure to hydrate well after the session.

For minor ailments and general health, one to a few sessions may show improvement. For chronic conditions, multiple sessions in a close time frame are recommended.

ATTRACT YOUR IDEAL BODY

Michelle Hastie

If you've ever been on a path to lose weight and get fit, you've probably been told and felt that you're not doing enough. With the quick pace of nutrition information and the ever-changing field of health and wellness, it can feel as though "doing enough" is impossible to maintain.

What's worse is many people may be doing "it all" and still not getting what they want. So they put their heads on their pillows at night wondering if they should be doing even more.

Thankfully, obtaining your ideal body is not a *doing* thing at all …

It's a *being* one.

The body is an incredible miracle machine that can heal broken bones, mend wounds, and even cure diseases. It keeps your heart beating and your food digesting, and it does all of this without any micromanaging. It's also responsible for burning fat and maintaining your ideal weight. And get this … it can do it all on its own! All you have to do is trust it and support it.

Regardless of how out of sync you may feel with your body, your mind is responsible for giving your body orders, including how many calories it burns and how it handles fat and nutrients. Seriously! There was a study conducted that illustrated this.

Participants were given identical milkshakes with competing labels. One label marked the first shake as indulgent and high fat, while the other marked the second shake as sensible and low calorie. While the ingredients in the shakes were identical, the bodies' responses to them were drastically different. The body released different hormones in response to drinking the different shakes — even in the same

> **We can trust our body is capable of being ideal and optimal, and that it has our full blessing to do so.**
>
> **We can be certain our body can digest and metabolize food at a rate that will burn fat and reduce its size.**
>
> **We can believe that food is a friend and exercise is a gift.**

person's body!

The hormonal response to the shakes wasn't the body's reaction, then. It was the mind's. And that brings about the question ... what is your mind telling your body to do?

Are you the person who jokingly states that looking at cake increases the size of your hips? Or that women like you don't get to eat cake and be thin? Or that only thin people get to indulge?

If we're thinking these thoughts, can we blame the body for obeying the orders we're giving it?

Just like we might use the Law of Attraction to bring in an ideal mate or job, we also can use this mindset to bring in our ideal body. Instead of thinking thoughts that sabotage our true desires, we can think (and believe) loving and supportive thoughts.

We can trust our body is capable of being ideal and optimal, and that it has our full blessing to do so.

We can be certain our body can digest and metabolize food at a rate that will burn fat and reduce its size.

We can believe that food is a friend and exercise is a gift.

Do you feel like it's a stretch to believe these things? Then you have a couple of options.

For the logical/analytical person: When you have unhelpful thoughts like, "Losing weight is hard for me" or "My body struggles with weight", imagine you are on a debate team and have to find evidence against those truths. Act as if it's your job to disprove those truths. Involve other people for different perspectives, and begin reducing the truth of those thoughts.

For the more emotional/feeling person: Record the beliefs that you want to believe, and in times when you are relaxed or in meditation, play them. Listen to them over and over again so your subconscious can hold on to them and allow them to replace the old ones.

Rather than trying to control your body through your actions, you can lead it to perform to the best of its ability with your thoughts. I encourage you to take a look at your mindset in regards to your body. Does it sync up with the positive messages you strive for in other areas? If not, how about trying something new?

Instead of focusing on doing this and doing that and simply doing so much more, be the person who loves and appreciates your body by showering it with praise and gratitude. Tell your body you love honoring it with delicious and nutritious food. Thank it for easily assimilating your pizza and beer on a Sunday afternoon.

Instead of waiting for what you're doing to get you what you want, start attracting what you want by being who you want to be. Be the person who listens to her body. Be the person you envision when you think of having your ideal body. Be that beautiful version of yourself that is free of the burden you feel when it comes to your weight and body. Be that person right now. And let your physical body show up as a result.

Michelle Hastie has expertise in personal training, food psychology, neuro-linguistic programming, and yoga. She is the author of *The Weight Loss Shift: Be More, Weigh Less*, *The Chakra Secret: What Your Body Is Telling You*, and *Have Your Cake and Be Happy, Too: A Joyful Approach to Weight Loss* and is a *Women Will Save the World* contributor. Visit www.totalbodyhealthsolutions.com.

SACRAL CHAKRA RECIPE

by Chef Maria Schonder

The sacral chakra is supported by water and, when balanced, keeps us juicy (at least that's how I think of it!) Since the sacral chakra is associated with our reproductive systems and our creativity, juicy and flowing is what we want!

One way to support your sacral chakra through food is enjoying those that are hydrating and have seeds (to represent fertility). If the food is orange in color, all the better!

CANTALOUPE SALAD

Makes 6-8 servings

Ingredients

2 ripe peaches, pits removed, peeled
¼ cup (scant) shallot
1 Tbsp chopped fresh tarragon
1 Tbsp fresh lime juice
Pinch salt
1 Tbsp extra virgin olive oil
1 cantaloupe, seeds removed, peeled, cut into 1-inch cubes

Directions

Coarsely chop the peaches, and add them to a food processor bowl.
Add shallot, tarragon, lime juice, and salt.
Puree while drizzling in olive oil until smooth.
Place cantaloupe in a large bowl. Top with dressing, stir well.
Serve immediately or refrigerate for up to 4 hours.

From Michelle Hastie's
The Chakra Secret: What Your Body Is Telling You, a min-e-book™

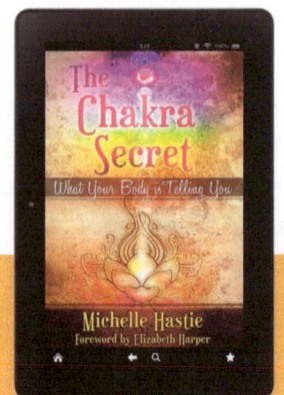

I am intuitive.

I acknowledge that I know what is best for me.

I acknowledge that all others know what is best for them.

I allow myself quiet time so my inner voice becomes clearer.

I notice physical symptoms and environmental cues, in order to clarify any intuitive messages I may not understand.

I recognize that I have access to the collective unconscious of all times, and I use this knowledge to assist me.

From Women Will Save the World

FENG SHUI FIXERS

PICK-ME-UPS FOR YOUR HOME

Create a nice view in one area where you spend time. Place a vibrant plant, wash a window, add a bouquet of flowers. Extend the view beyond the interior, and spruce up the lawn or plants on the exterior, too. Create a haven where you can look and relax, and this will bring more peace into your home.

Clear out underneath a bed. It is said that when energy gets stuck underneath a bed, it affects our ability to sleep well. Do you really need all those boxes? Clear them out to declutter but also to improve your sleep. While you're at it, borrow someone's electronic vacuum for the day to reach the spots you're not able to reach.

Speaking of vacuuming, vacuum the floor. Everything we drop, literally and energetically, resides on the floor. Running a vacuum will eliminate those things that drag us down and will make a room feel energized. This is great for a quick pick-me-up!

Add a crystal to a sunny window, and let the sunlight add a rainbow sparkle. Crystals are affordable and an easy way to bring in the bounty of the sun's goodness. They are said to break up bad energy wherever they reflect and to bring in lots of good. Plus, the reflections are pretty!

You've heard it before: declutter. While we might think having lots of things around us is comforting, it actually brings us down, as our brain constantly registers everything in our presence, whether we realize it or not. Look where you are sitting. In your view, what uplifts you? What is neutral, and what brings you down? Put away (or give away) anything that is not uplifting.

Fix a ding. It's not realistic to have a "perfect" house, but find one small task or a dent or a chip, and fix that. Once it's done, you'll realize how much you thought about it each time you walked by. Now, it's not there anymore to "ding" your energy!

LAW OF CORRESPONDENCE

The **Universal Law of Correspondence** says that what we think about, we create. What this means is that if we want to change something in our external world, we have to first change our inner world.

What are you spending your time thinking about today, and how could you change your thoughts to create a better day? Here are a few ideas to help the results of the Law of Correspondence feel more rewarding in your life:

Replace a self-criticism with a praise. Whatever setbacks or challenges you may be facing, you are doing *something* well. Focus on that.

Replace a worry with a best-case thought. It can be easy to let worries bring you down, but it also can be easy to let aspirational thoughts bring you up. Most things we worry about simply don't manifest anyway so think of the best-case scenario for how a situation you are facing today could unfold, whether it's a meeting at your child's school or a decision that could change the trajectory of your life.

Focus on your higher intentions. During an average day, we have thousands of thoughts about getting from one moment to the next: things to do, where to go, etc. We obviously want to function well with our day-to-day tasks, but don't allow yourself to be so consumed with menial thoughts that you lose track of the bigger picture.

Stop re-working old conversations. Maybe you had an argument, maybe you snapped at someone, or maybe you just missed an opportunity to say something that would have been helpful, but now you're stewing over it. Change your focus. It happened, acknowledge it, let the guilt go, and do your best to fix it.

Feed yourself with positive media. Whether it's books or the nightly news or television shows, what goes in, goes out!

Taking any of these small, daily steps will help the life you experience be a happier one. After all, smile at yourself, and the world will smile back at you!

GET BACK ON TRACK

What will help you get back on track to creating a better inside world so you can create a better outside world? Pick the number that feels best to you now, without peeking at the below text. Then, see what action will help you re-center yourself for the most positive day possible.

One: Get in some water! Take a sea salt bath, go for a swim, take a walk by a lake or pond or ocean. Even take a shower or splash water on your face to clear away any picked-up negativity.

Two: Take a nap. Even if you only can swing a 10-minute refresh, go get horizontal and give your brain and body a chance to re-boot.

Three: Take a breather, and put your mind on pause. Try a five-minute meditation, or read something that feels good to help clear away some of your swirling thoughts.

ATTENTION, LIBRARY LOVERS!

Did you know you can request that any of the Absolute Love Publishing books be purchased by your local library? For most library systems, it's as easy as filling out a short online form. Contact your library today to request our books, and help yourself and other patrons enjoy them for years to come!

You never do anything that is not in some way an attempt to bring more light into your life.

From Personal Power through Awareness by Sanaya Roman

You were born with potential. You were born with goodness and trust. You were born with ideals and dreams. You were born with greatness. You were born with wings.

You are not meant for crawling, so don't. You have wings. Learn to use them and fly. - Rumi

An Angelic Message

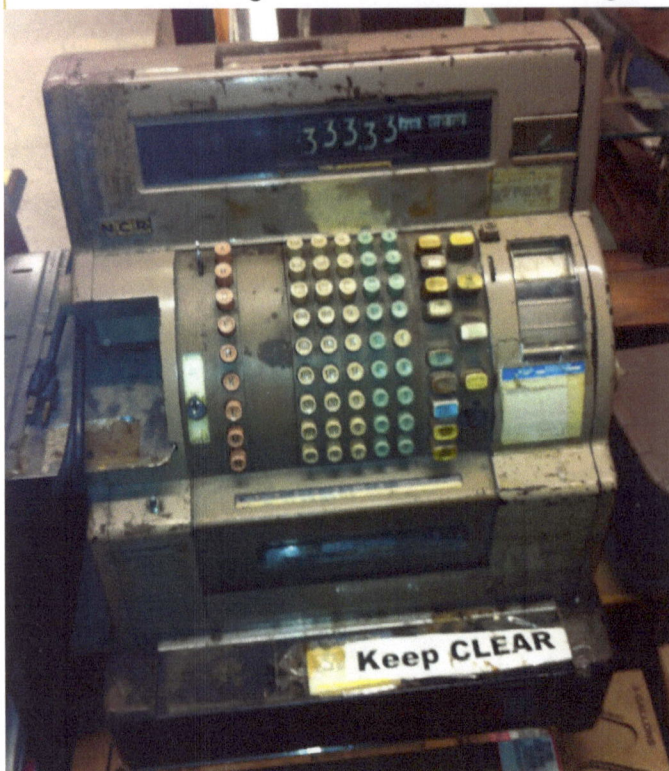

On the 333rd day of a Leap Year, with 33 days left, I felt energy crackling around me. Was it real? I asked my angels for a sign that I had recognized something special and felt, almost watched, that intention melt into the air. Minutes later, I strolled into an old-fashioned soda shop, and here is what I found! Consider it a hello and a message from my angels, to you: **Keep clear in your thoughts, your heart, your mind, your time, and your space.**
- Absolute Love Publishing Founder
Caroline A. Shearer

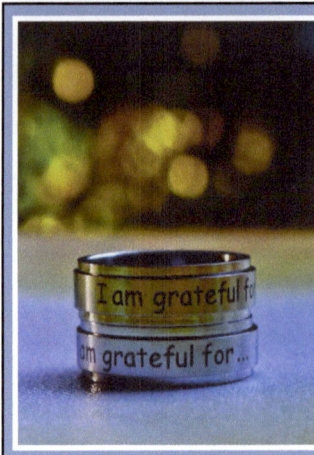
BOOK CLUBS & MORE

Are you in a book club? Absolute Love Publishing offers discounts for bulk purchases, including for book clubs and organizations. We also offer incentive bonuses, such as online Q&A's with the author with a minimum purchase.

Visit our online store to see what options are publicly available, and/or email us for more information on how you can qualify for a discount or a bonus.

Store: www.absolutelovepublishing.com/shop
Email: publisher@absolutelovepublishing.com

LOVE ALOVEDLIFE?

Be sure to read every edition of this evergreen publication! Check our store, and sign up for our emails to catch each issue!

ATTENTION, TEACHERS & SCHOOLS!

What better way to promote a love of reading and writing than to host an author at your school? The Absolute Love Publishing authors are available for both in-person and Skype visits, and we can work with you to create the best outcome for your students. Contact ambassador@absolutelovepublishing.com today!

MIDDLE GRADE BOOKS

YOUNG ADULT BOOKS

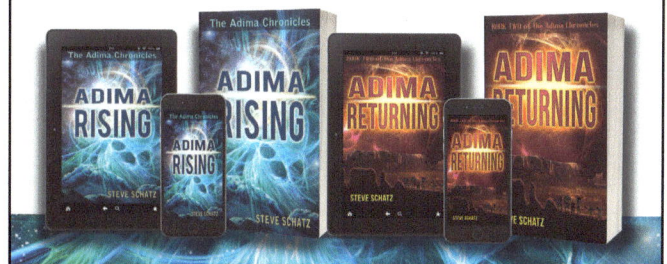

Be kind to yourself. You are doing your best.